A Wake Up Call

Gary S. Hall

A Wake Up Call

A Coming to Know God

A Wake Up Call
Copyright © 2009 by Gary S. Hall. All rights reserved.
Re-Published by Redemption Press in 2017, PO Box 427, Enumclaw, WA 98022
Toll Free (844) 2REDEEM (273-3336)

Redemption Press is honored to present this title in partnership with the author. The views expressed or
implied in this work are those of the author. Redemption Press provides our imprint seal representing
design excellence, creative content and high quality production.

No part of this publication may be reproduced, stored in a retrieval system, or transmitted in any way by any means—electronic, mechanical, photocopy, recording, or otherwise—without the prior permission of the copyright holder, except as provided by USA copyright law.

All Scripture quotations are taken from the Holy Bible, King James Version, Cambridge, 1769. Used by permission. All rights reserved.

Published in the United States of America

ISBN: 978-1-68314-584-4

Acknowledgements

I want to acknowledge, first and foremost, God. I give you all of the honor and glory. Thank you for the healing power of the spirit.

Thanks to my mom and dad for seeing that my brother and I were brought up in a home where God was presented to us from birth.

I would like to express a special thank you to Dr. Wayne Dyer, a person whom I have never met but feel as though we are one. Dr. Dyer, Namaste.

H. P. Thank you for your patience and understanding. I love you, man!

I would also like to thank all of you, and you know who you are, that have recognized and acknowledged the presence of God in your own lives and have written about the evidence and expression of God's manifestation for all of humanity. Thank you all.

I would also like thank all of the medical doctors and specialists that I have seen during my bout with Epstein-Barr that said that there is no cure for this and it would have to run its course.

My wife, Jami, I do not yet know the words to express the depth of gratitude that I have for your patience, love, kindness, and understanding since we have been together but especially during Epstein. I love you.

Table of Contents

Introduction	9	Maintaining Contact	67
Past Medical History	15	Prayer/Meditation	75
Epstein-Barr virus	23	Manifesting	79
My Epstein-Barr	37	Bibliography	91
Initial Contact	51		
Doubt	58		
Ego	60		
Our Past	64		

Introduction

You have found yourself looking at this book and contemplating its purchase. You are thinking several things: first, I have never heard of this author, who is he? Second, is it worth the money, and third, and most importantly, is it worth the time I will spend reading it?

The answer to the first question will follow, but the answer to the time and money question is this. You will get out of it what you put into it, meaning I *know* that if you will read this book and put into practice the things taught, you will have a better life and a life more abundant. Now I don't mean read it put it down and never look at it again. I mean, read it, study it, live it. Come to know God and have a life more abundant!

The answer to the first question is this: my name is Gary Hall. I was born in Nashville, Tennessee on May 20, 1966. I was born to wonderful parents, Terry and Margie Hall, who were originally from the Macon county area in northern, middle Tennessee. I have one brother, Brent, who is almost six years *older* than I am.

I had your typical middle-class childhood: great neighborhood, nice house, good friends. It was wonderful, well, most of the time. The other times, I battled a multitude of injuries, illnesses, and surgeries. I speak of these in detail in the first chapter.

In my early twenties, I was overtaken by my own ego, and it cost me almost everything I had. You can read more of this later in the book as well.

Then at forty, I was diagnosed with Epstein-Barr virus. It took several months of living with this dis-ease before I came to the realization that I didn't have to. I didn't have to deal with any dis-ease, dis-harmony, discord or anything of the like. I knew God, and that was all I had to know. God.

In regards to my credentials: I am forty-two years old. I am an electrician by trade. I am now the director of operations for a large electrical contractor based in Nashville, Tennessee. I have been married three times. I have four wonderful children and three grandchildren.

Miranda is my oldest daughter, eighteen, by my first wife. Dylan, age twelve, and Haley, age eleven, by my second wife. Rob, my stepson, is thirty-four, and he has three beautiful children, Lauren, age eleven, Tucker, age six and (Mini) Cooper, age three. These grandchildren are by and through my third and final marriage to Jami.

I have no formal education of which to speak. I did attend Nashville Technical Institute but only for one year. I tell people who ask, I received my education at the school of Hard Shocks. Looking back, Mom and Dad, you were right; it would have been much easier to have stayed in school.

I was saved by the grace of God at the age of nine, and I remember immediately after the Spirit entered that I had this knowing that I had to tell others of this experience. I immediately got up and walked out of the church and told the first person I saw, a friend of mine by the name of Jimmy Sutton and then a cousin, Eric Fleming. The next day I told my next-door neighbor Barry Wiss.

As time passed my consciousness became clouded with life, and I guess you could say I lost my focus. I have had moments throughout my life of slipping in and out of this higher consciousness or God consciousness. I don't know maybe you have too. But at these times of higher consciousness, if you'll think about it,

11   *A Wake Up Call*

you are more at peace. You are healthier, happier, and more content. The struggles of life seem to vanish and true living begins.

When we live in and through the Spirit, we can have an abundant life full of health and anything else we would like to manifest into our lives. I have not always followed the Spirit as I should have, but it has always followed me, regardless of if I have been receptive to It or not. And let me say, not only does it follow you, it is in front of you, beside you, and in everything around you. As a matter of fact, it is you. You may not acknowledge and may not want to acknowledge the fact that the Spirit is you, but that is exactly what you and we are. We are spirit.

I have not always thought on these terms, but since I was a child, it seems as though everything in my life has led me to the writing of this book. In Romans, it says all things work together for good to them that love God. As I look back on my life, I now see those surgeries and all of the illnesses as blessings. Even the knockdown drag-outs I had with my own ego were all stepping-stones leading me to now. If you are reading this, your stepping-stones have led you to this book, now, as well.

So you could say, this book has been forty-two years, countless people, and numerous experiences in the making. This includes you. Thank you. I don't claim to be a great author, a great speaker, or anything of the like. As you have read, I have had no formal education. But I do now know this, I am. I am that which God hath made. I am spirit and you are too. We have been given dominion over everything including, first and foremost, our mind and body. It is time to reclaim this dominion, maintain higher levels of consciousness, and manifest into your life anything you wish.

Read, Believe, and Live

Past Medical History

(As You Think, So Shall You Be)

Let us begin by looking at my past medical history. It is extremely important for you to know this history, and that I didn't just suddenly contract Epstein-Barr, get over it, and write a book. My entire life has led me here and yours has too. So let us begin.

My first surgery was having my tonsils and adenoids removed at age three. At age five, I had double hernias surgically repaired. From the time I was five until I was thirteen, I was chronically ill. I don't know why, and doctors couldn't tell us either, but I stayed sick. It seemed as though I was continuously coming down with one thing or another and running high fevers for no apparent reason.

***

This is the time where I have some of the fondest memories of my mom. Not only was she the taxi to take my brother and me everywhere we went, but she was always by my side. I remember countless days and nights that I would be sick, and she would be right there with a cold washcloth rubbing my forehead, or she would be in other rooms of the house doing housework while talking to God and pleading for my speedy recovery. My mom used to always say that after death if people remembered her as a Christian, her life had been a success. Mom can't hear me say it now nor does she need to; however, I will say it anyway. Mom, you were a success.

***

Now being sick so frequently you can only imagine the bloodletting. I was constantly having blood drawn and sent to this lab and that lab in states all across the country. There were times I felt like a human pincushion. These tests would typically show a high white blood count or a low white blood count and that's all—nothing more and nothing less. I think the doctors were thinking that at anytime that there was going to be something that would just jump right out at them and solve the mystery. After many of these pricks and pokes, they decided there must be something wrong with my thyroid, so they took a piece of it out and tested that too. This was surgery number four. Seven days later, I was rushed back to the operating room for what doctors originally thought was probably appendicitis, but during surgery, they found I had ruptured my lower intestines.

The injury happened during a horse-riding incident at my aunt and uncle's house two days before I fell ill. My cousin and I saddled up our horses and were ready to go. The horse I rode was a follower, and it would always follow my cousin's horse. This would get extremely aggravating.

Before I could get saddled, my cousin had taken off. Of course, my horse suddenly took off. I had my left leg in the stirrup, my left hand on reins, and my right hand on the saddle horn. About time I threw my right leg over the horse, my cousin had turned around to see this poetry in motion and stopped. Now I told you that the horse I was on was a follower, but I didn't tell you that he was a stopper as well. When my cousin's horse stopped, my horse would stop on a dime, and I mean at a dead run too. So when my right leg was over the horse, he came to screeching halt and my lower right abdomen hit the saddle horn. It didn't hurt too badly, so we went on about our riding. The next day I woke up not feeling very well, but thought I was only saddle sore. The following day I had surgery number five.

After number five, I went three years without a surgery. Of course, I still had the typical sprained ankle, broken fingers, elbows—the normal kid-growing-up-doing-martial-arts-in-the-woods type of stuff.

At age sixteen, I had my first knee surgery—right knee scoped. This was due to being chased by a couple of girls while working our sophomore homecoming float. Then at nineteen, I had a water skiing incident and had to have my left knee scoped.

At the age of twenty-three, I was hospitalized for rectal bleeding and severe cramps. They performed various tests, several of which required the use of cameras that they would send down my throat, up my nose, and finally up my ... well you get the picture. It's called a colonoscopy. They found polyps during this test. I had a CAT scan the next day, and they noticed a mass on

Gary S. Hall

my left lung. The doctors decided the mass in my lung was a more potential problem than the polyps, so they suggested we remove the lower lobe of my left lung. Then after healing from this surgery, we would worry about the polyps in my colon. The healing process took about three to four months to get back to normal activities and about a year before I wanted to take any kind of impact to that side of my body. By this time, I was having no further problems with my colon. After this surgery, I went about eleven years without one.

Next, I had the rotator cuff in my left shoulder repaired at age thirty-four and another hernia on my right side at age thirty-five. My last surgery was to try to remove a fragment of bone that kept floating around my hand at age thirty-nine.

Then on September 18, 2006, my mother had double knee replacements. The knee replacements went well, but the doctors failed to evaluate my mother for any possible allergic reactions to blood thinners. The heparin they gave her to thin the blood had worked just the opposite. It was clotting everywhere.

She was on life support for the last three days of her life. When there was no more brain activity, the family

19   *A Wake Up Call*

made the decision to remove the life support and let her pass. She would not have wanted to lie there lifeless. Mom died on October 5, 2006, at 10:30 a.m. The one thing I'll never forget. I was standing over her just after she passed, and I felt her spirit pass right through me on its final journey home.

I had felt God's spirit before and I had felt God's spirit in others before, but this was different. It was as if my mom's spirit took the place of my own spirit. It filled me up. I should have felt sad due to her passing and did later, but at that moment, I wanted to shout with exhilaration, my mom's spirit had passed through me before going to God.

You just read the majority of my medical history and some personal stuff, as well. The reason for this is that I want you to see my record, if you will... my history. My entire life seemed to be filled with sickness, surgery, and injury. I remember thinking, *Well, I'm okay now, but I wonder what's coming next. Would it be a cold or flu? Would it be a sprain or broken bone? Or would it be some kind of surgery?* After my mom's death, about a month before Epstein, I remember saying to Jami, "I wonder what is going to happen next?"

I had set myself up for failure before it ever happened, and I had been my entire life, moving from this sickness to this injury to that surgery and so on.

What we must do is change the way we think. Buddha put it this way: All that we are is the result of what we have thought. The mind is everything. What we think, we become. Solomon, another extremely wise man, says in the book of Proverbs, "For as he thinketh in his heart, so is he."

Epstein-Barr Virus

(The Beginning)

Jami and I had gone to Destin, Florida, for New Year's just to have a long, quiet weekend together. We try to get down there three or four times a year just to get away and relax. It was New Year's, so we were going to go to all of our favorite places to eat: The Back Porch, Pompano Joe's, AJ's, etc. We told ourselves we could eat whatever we wanted because it was about to be a new year, and in 2007 we were going to get more strict with our diet, work out more—all of the things you always say as a New Year approaches.

We were having a wonderful weekend together and woke up one morning, and suddenly, it was January 1,

2007. My, how time flies. It was a beautiful morning. Jami and I moved to the balcony to have the first cup of coffee of the morning and watch the almost motionless emerald green waters drift lazily to the beach. We did this every morning we were there. It was just so peaceful. However, something was different about this morning. My body was telling me something was wrong. It felt like maybe a cross between a possible flu bug or maybe a stomach virus. I was just not feeling like myself. My first thought was it was something I ate the night before or maybe it was that I just hadn't worked out in a few days. I finally dismissed it and went on about the day.

Jami and I both worked out at least three days a week, but in 2007 I was going to get on a *get big* routine. I had told Jami that I was going to turn forty-one in May, and I wanted to be as strong as I had ever been by that day. We drove back from Destin to Nashville the afternoon of January 1, and I was really excited about getting started on this new exercise routine.

I have exercised in some fashion since I was thirteen

years old. At thirteen, some friends, and I worked out by doing martial arts, studying different styles from kung fu to karate and also trying to read anything by Stephen Hayes, the founder of To Shin Do with a Home Dojo located in Dayton, Ohio.

We would go into the woods and train for hours. My backyard looked like some kind of training ground for the CIA. We had three trampolines, rolling mats, and a carousel that held heavy bags. We would jump, flip, dive roll, and battle with anything we could pick up. It basically looked like one of those crazy movies you used to watch, the ones where their lips moved and then a few seconds later you hear their voice.

At nineteen, I had another friend John Lee introduce me to weight training. I loved it. No matter where I have lived, traveled, or worked, I have always had to find a gym to work out. In the beginning, like most people starting out, I wanted to get as big as a house. I tried to for years, using all manner of vitamins, supplements, and anything that said it would make you big.

Now, I realize it's more important to maintain a more well-rounded approach to fitness based on the physical, emotional, and spiritual aspect of our lives.

We arrived back home on January 2, and I started this *get big* routine. I had wonderful results. I would work chest and triceps on Monday, shoulders and biceps on Tuesday, and legs and back on Wednesday. Also, I would ride a stationary bike twenty minutes prior to lifting and would alternate the abs and calves every other day. I was taking three different kinds of supplements, all legal.

And don't forget the diet; I put myself on a protein only diet. I was eating five to six times and drinking a gallon of water every day. I really thought I had it going on, but at times I would get that feeling I had that morning in Destin, that feeling of something was just not right.

The workouts continued throughout January and into February. I had said I was going to be as strong as I had ever been, and I was on my way. My bench press (it seems like everybody judges their strength by the bench press) by the end of January was 225 pounds for ten, on January 2, when I had started, it was 185 pounds for eight. Although, I never really was that strong compared to most of the guys I've worked out with, but for me I was really getting it back.

It was the second week of February, and Jami came

down with the flu. I couldn't believe it, this woman was never sick, never felt bad, nothing. I mean, she was like made of steel all four foot eleven inches of her. Thankfully, we caught it early, went to the doctor, and got the proper medication. Jami was down for about a week but bounced back rather quickly. The whole time I was thinking, *I sure hope she gets over this quick.* Right? No, really I was thinking, *I sure hope I don't get this mess. I've got a great routine going, and I don't want to mess it up and potentially lose what I have gained.* A week passed, and I was feeling fine. I was thinking, *Man, I'm in the clear.*

Tuesday morning, February 20, 2007, it hit. The day I will never forget. Just one day prior, Monday, I had worked chest and triceps. I was bench-pressing 250 pounds for sets of twelve, absolutely as strong as I had ever been. I woke up that morning and couldn't raise my head off the pillow. At first, I'm thinking, *Okay, here we go, my turn, I've got the flu. It finally hit.* With this in mind I thought, *Well, I might as well get up and push through it.* I struggled to get out of bed and went down stairs to the gym. I thought I would try to do something, anything, just keep working. I didn't want to lose anything I had gained; what a mind set. I couldn't lift a twenty-pound dumbbell, so I decided to give it up for the day. I thought I would make an attempt to proceed with the day and I did.

It was my mother-in-law's birthday, so after work, the family had dinner at a Japanese restaurant. My oldest daughter was also playing in a championship basketball game that night about an hour away from our home, and I made it to that as well. But by the time the game is over, I was feeling like I had been hit in the head with a sledgehammer.

I woke the next morning, Wednesday, and didn't feel quite as bad, I thought well, just maybe I had dodged a bullet and wasn't going to get the full-blown flu. Then came Thursday. I woke up not knowing what to think. I didn't feel too terrible, but I couldn't say how I felt. It didn't feel like the flu. Or was it?

I wasn't running a fever, but I had woken up with this aching pain in my ankles and an ache in my low abdomen. Later in the day, around noon, I had a meeting at a jobsite that I had to attend. While driving to this meeting, I began to get dizzy and was swerving all over the road. This was different. I have had the flu but never felt like this. I pulled to the shoulder of the road and made the call. I called my doctors office and asked if they could work me in and they did.

I arrived at the doctor's office around three o'clock that afternoon. I was seen promptly and described to my doctor the symptoms that I had been having throughout the week and that now the same pain that I had been experiencing in my ankles this morning was in my knees as well. After my explanation and his examination, he thought that I probably had a problem with my prostate. I was diagnosed with a prostate infection that would last a few days to a week, given a prescription, and sent home.

A week came and went. There had been no sign of getting any better, and as a matter of fact, by that weekend I thought that I definitely had the flu. I could hardly function. That next Thursday I returned to my doctor and explained my symptoms and now the pain that had been in ankles and knees had now worked its way to my hips, shoulders, and neck down to my elbows and wrist. On this visit, I wasn't really diagnosed with anything. They were just not sure. It could still be the prostate infection, flu, or something else. The problem was I didn't have a fever and my outward appearance was great. The doctor and his staff, along with everybody else, would always comment, "You may feel bad, but you look great." I must say that it would just infuriate me to no end to hear this, but I guess all of that working out in January and February had paid off.

Another week goes by, and there's no sign of getting any better and now the joint pain had turned into muscle aches and spasms. Now I'm thinking, *Man, I'm really falling apart.*

I go back to the doctor for more poking and prodding. On this visit, the blood work began, as did talks of rheumatoid arthritis or possibly some sort of muscular dystrophy. *Now I'm getting a little worried.*

Over the next few weeks, I had to see several specialists for different testing. All of these tests came back negative. I didn't have rheumatoid arthritis or any type of muscular dystrophy. I was relieved but still worried, confused, and worst of all sick.

I am sure anyone who has ever had a long-time illness can relate. I had been sick now for over a month, and I don't mean just a bad cold or just not feeling very well. I mean days on end of not being able to function. There were days that I could hardly raise my head off the pillow much less get out of bed. It was really beginning to take its toll. I began to think, *Is this the end? Am I dying?* There were those days that I would have welcomed death in my weak and feeble state of mind.

On another occasion, Jami had to pick me up at my office and take me to Vanderbilt University Hospital emergency room because I thought I was going to die. Once we arrived, they conducted the typical emergency room stuff. They made sure I wasn't going to die, told me I looked great, and sent me home telling me I was fine.

It wasn't just taking its toll on me; it was hurting everyone, especially my wife. She was the one who had to listen to my moaning and groaning, morning and night. In the past, we had typically split all of the domestic duties around the house, and now she had to do everything.

Jami and I could talk for hours about nothing other than how much we loved each other. It was and is amazing. Now we hardly spoke, unless it was about this ailment I had or how bad it was that day. I couldn't participate in our children or grandchildren's activities. This thing I had, whatever it was, was merciless. It took its toll on everyone.

And let's not forget my co-workers. There would be days that I didn't go in to work because I couldn't get out of bed and then there were the days I would leave early or soon after my arrival because I couldn't stay up any longer.

I just had to figure it out. I continued to go and see my doctor sometimes twice a day just knowing that I was going to die if we didn't figure this thing out. I remember, probably the second week of April now, going to his office and throwing myself at his mercy, and begging him to please find out what was going on. I told him that I thought I was losing my mind. He was ever so gracious listening to my plea. When I had finished, he agreed. "It had been long enough," he said. "We need to find out what this thing is." He got me back in the office the next morning for more blood work. This time we checked for everything, he even checked for HIV/AIDS. I was told I would have to sign a release, which I was glad to do. I just had to know what was going on.

This entire time I had whatever it was I had, I had never been given any kind of medication, except for the prostate stuff, which I quit taking shortly after I started. My doctor had told me he didn't want to medicate something he didn't know how to medicate, and I agreed.

After the last bloodletting, I thought, *I had better do something.* I had the "if you want to get something

Gary S. Hall   32

done, you might as well do it yourself" attitude. So for the first time in months, I had finally taken a step in the right direction and called my chiropractor. He got me in on April 27, 2007 at eleven o'clock. I was excited about the appointment.

I have a wonderful chiropractor, Dr. Paul Perceddu. He has such a gentle adjustment technique. I would recommend Dr. Perceddu to anyone who needed a great chiropractor.

I was so excited about this visit to my chiropractor that Jami wanted to go. Jami had been with me through this whole thing, went to other doctors' appointments, and had taken me to the emergency room on occasion, so it was only fitting that she went to this visit as well.

On the way to this appointment, I told Jami, "This is it. This is the day for healing; it starts today." Well, as we were pulling into the parking lot of Dr. P's office, my cell phone rang; it was my medical doctor. It had been about a week to a week and a half since the last bloodletting, so I'm thinking, *It's about time.*

The nurse said, "Mr. Hall, we have results back from your blood work, and it has been confirmed with three tests, you have Epstein-Barr virus."

I said, "What in the world is Epstein-Barr virus?" She began to tell me what it was, and I was ecstatic.

I had wanted to know for months what in the world is going on and now I knew. It was wonderful. Well, it was for just a moment. After she finished explaining Epstein-Barr virus (EBV), I said, "Well that's great! "Now what?" I asked.

"Well, Mr. Hall," she said, "I'm sorry, but there is nothing more we can do. We wish we could help, but there is no known cure; it will just have to run its course. Now if you have anything else happen please come back and see us, but with the EBV, there is nothing we can do." I believe she was trying to say in a nice way, *Don't come back*.

Well, I did have other things happen: my EBV kept on hitting me with new symptoms. I would have aching muscles one day, joint pain the next, flu-like symptoms, sometimes just plain ole fatigue. Some days I just couldn't get out of bed. There were days of vomiting and upset stomach and the most recent symptom was when I was sitting in my office somewhere around the middle of September, and I started seeing tracers in my right eye. I went to the eye doctor who sent me to a specialist who ran a bunch of tests; these tests all came back negative. This doctor asked if I had been having any other problems. I explained the past months of dealing with EBV. When he heard this, I would have thought I had just cursed at him, shot his dog, or kicked his cat. I saw the look. He was done talking to me. He and his assistant both told me they were finished, and if I had no further questions, I was free to go. They exited the room with no further explanation.

You've read my medical history, some of my symptoms with EBV, my experience with doctors with EBV. Now, what do you say let's be done with all of this negative talk about what was. Let us now talk for just a moment about what Epstein-Barr is, the course of action I took trying to get over it, and, finally, the solution to Epstein-Barr and not only Epstein-Barr, but I believe, the solution or answer, if you will, to life.

My Epstein-Barr

(The Search for a Cure)

What is Epstein-Barr virus (EBV)?

Epstein-Barr virus, an autoimmune disease, frequently referred to as EBV, is a member of the herpes virus family and one of the most common human viruses. The virus occurs worldwide, and most people become infected with EBV sometime during their lives. In the United States as many as ninety-five percent of adults between thirty-five and forty years of age have been infected. Infants become susceptible to EBV as soon as maternal antibody protection (present at birth) disappears. Many children become infected with EBV, and these infections usually cause no symptoms or are indistinguishable from the other mild, brief illnesses of childhood.

Symptoms of Epstein-Barr virus most commonly are fatigue, and foggy headedness. Epstein-Barr can be very disabling and can result in someone being so tired that they cannot get out of bed. Sometimes, a swollen spleen or liver involvement may develop. Heart problems or involvement of the central nervous system occurs only rarely, and infectious mononucleosis is almost never fatal. Although symptoms of infectious mononucleosis usually resolve in one to two months, there have been cases in older adults that symptoms can last up to eighteen months. EBV remains dormant or latent in a few cells in the throat and blood for the rest of the person's life. Periodically, the virus can reactivate and is commonly found in the saliva of infected persons. This reactivation usually occurs without symptoms of illness. Epstein-Barr can reoccur at any time, especially after illness or stress.

As I had said in the last chapter, it was Friday April 27, 2007, and I had an appointment with my chiropractor. I had just been told I had EBV. Now prior to my doctor's phone call, I had never heard of Epstein-Barr. I walked into Dr. Porceddu's office. I had been a patient of Dr. P's for several years, so at first, we had the typical chatting then moved right into what's going on. I told him I had just been diagnosed with EBV, and what can he do to help.

He said, "You are not going to believe this, but I've had EBV." He began to explain the symptoms he had had, and guess what? They were some of the same symptoms I had been having. I couldn't believe it, one minute I'm feeling all alone not knowing what to do with this stuff I've never heard of, and the next, I've got someone that can relate to how I'm feeling.

Dr. P explained that he had EBV in his mid-twenties and that he had struggled as well. He also explained how chiropractic treatment could ease some of the symptoms and also assist in the cure through relieving pressure on specific nerves during the adjustment procedures. After the adjustment, Dr. P continued to instruct me on things to do to combat this EBV. I left his office with a most wonderful feeling, thinking, *Now, I am on my way.* Until the next day. I was then back down again, just as sick as I had ever been. This occurred throughout the rest of my search.

The next week, and for many weeks, Jami and I discussed different options. There were clinics in Mexico and Cleveland Clinic and Mayo Clinic here in the states that we thought about trying. I had my second visit with Dr. Perceddu that next Friday. At this visit, I explained that I had felt all right on Friday night, but after that, the whole week I was shot. He stated that I needed to get additional support. He suggested that I go see, if they could get me in, Belle Meade Health and Wellness Clinic. He also stated that this clinic would treat things that your medical doctor would say are untreatable thru methods that they would turn their nose up to. This was my first experience with alternative or holistic medicines.

I continued my chiropractic visits and started at Belle Meade Health and Wellness (BMHW) the last week of May. This was where I met Linn Strouse. She was a licensed RN and ran the clinic. We started my treatment with a series of colonics or colonic irrigation.

What is a colonic irrigation? Colonic irrigation is also known as hydrotherapy of the colon, high colonic, or simply colonic. It is the process of cleansing the colon by passing several gallons of water through it with the use of special equipment. It is similar to an enema but treats the whole colon, not just the lower bowel. This has the effect of flushing out impacted fecal matter, toxins, mucous, and even parasites that often build up over the passage of time. It is a procedure that should only be undertaken by a qualified practitioner.

Linn also put me on a strict diet, no bread or gluten,

no sugar, no milk or dairy products and no red meat. *That means no steak*. What would I do? This meant an entire new way of eating. This was going to be as tough as the EBV, but I was determined that I was going to beat this thing. And don't let me forget the vitamins, minerals, and herbs. I was taking some twenty-two vitamins, minerals, and herbs, sometimes three times a day.

After a few visits, I was getting some better but not a huge difference. Linn suggested that we try the Quantum Xeroid Consciousness Interface (QXCI), and we did. This was remarkable. In layman's terms, the QXCI sends, throughout your body, a very small electrical current to evaluate all of the frequencies that all of your systems are running at. Everything in our body operates at a certain frequency, and the QXCI is designed to know these frequencies and has therapy programs that can correct any deficiencies. Everything in this universe has a frequency, from solid objects to your thoughts to the spirit.

Linn told me that for the first three minutes the machine would run a scan of my entire body, every system, everything, and would report back its findings. What Linn proceeded to tell me was astonishing. Linn had only known me for a few weeks, and she did not have my personal medical records from birth, but she began to tell me things that had happened to me from birth and things that would not have been in my medical records anyway. It was simply, or not so simply, amazing.

She told me that I was allergic to chocolate. I explained that I had been allergic to chocolate when I was a child but had outgrown it. Linn said, "No you haven't. You have just acquired a tolerance for it." She asked, "Do you have any trouble breathing?"

I said no.

She said, "Well, according to this, you have less capacity in one lung."

She knew of broken bones and all sorts of traumas through this machine. Later in the test, she checked my aura. This was pretty amazing as well. My aura was a light blue, and after a few seconds, it exploded into this brilliant white light, Linn seemed to be overwhelmed and pushed herself away from her desk, and asked, "Do you pray?"

I said, "Well of course I pray, probably not as much as I should, but I do pray."

She then asked, "Do you meditate?"

I said, "I did when I was younger but haven't in years. I had never received any training. I would just focus on what I wanted to accomplish, it seemed to help, but I wasn't very disciplined in my practice."

She then asked *the question*, "What do you think

your purpose is?" I had never really thought about it. She asked, "If I would start meditating, I have never seen an aura like this before, as sick as you are it should be red or something other than white." She further explained that the white aura typically is related to the spirit and that I had something that I must do and that I really needed to figure it out. I said, half heartily, "Oh, yeah, that's great … really?"

I continued to see Linn through July, and at every visit she would ask, "Are you mediating yet?"

I would explain, "No, not yet. I'm very busy. I just really don't have the time."

Linn would say, "Remember you have something to do. Be about it." She also asked, "When do you listen to God?" This was an amazing question. Nobody had ever asked me that.

I wanted to say, *Well, all the time*, but that would have been a lie. So instead I said, "You know, not near enough."

She said, "That is why you must meditate. When we pray is when we talk to God and when we meditate is when we listen to what God is saying to us."

I, once again, half heartily said, "Oh, yeah, that's great … really?"

It wasn't until the third week of August that I finally

took action on Linn's request. I thought to myself, *If I'm going to do this I want to do it right.* I got online and did some research on meditation and different home study courses, and I wound up at the Silva Ultra Mind Web site. I downloaded the free home study course trial and tried it. I downloaded this information around ten o'clock that morning and started practicing right away. The first exercise was the centering exercise or the long relax. This was a guided relaxation technique and took approximately twenty-five minutes. I tried it, and thirty minutes later, I felt great. The meditation seemed to have worked. I started meditating at least twice a day and some days three times. I continued with this every day, but with the meditation alone, I was still having bad days. I could push through them with the help of meditation; nevertheless, they were still bad days. There was still something missing. It wasn't the meditation's fault I was still having bad days, it was my own.

It wasn't until December 5, 2007 that I realized what was missing. I had tried everything humanly possible to beat EBV, but that was the problem. I was turning to this doctor or that doctor, this herb or that, vitamins, supplements, etc. I was looking out, and I should have been looking within.

Gary S. Hall

On December 4 of 2007, Jami went to have her haircut. I know you're thinking, *What in the world has this got to do with anything?* At this visit, her stylist, Charlene Hall, gave her an audio CD by Dr. Wayne Dyer. Jami and Charlene are good friends, and she knew that I had been ill and thought that listening to the CD might provide some comfort or some assistance in my illness. Jami gave me this CD that evening. I told Jami to tell Charlene thanks and also that I will definitely listen to it. And listen to it I did.

Now, I had heard of Dr. Dyer before and had also caught his specials on public television when they were on. However, I had never purchased any of his material. I guess you could say I've listened to him, but I had never heard what he had to say. On the morning of December 5, I heard.

It was around six o'clock that morning, and I was driving to the office. I began to listen to the CD, *The Secrets of Your Own Healing Power*. I hadn't been listening very long. I was just nine minutes and thirty-nine seconds into the second track, when Dr. Dyer said something that really touched the deepest most inner part of my being.

He was relating a story about when he and his wife were visiting a small village in Bali, and they came across a man gazing up at the clouds. Dr. Dyer asked their guide what this gentleman was doing, and the guide replied that this man was a cloud mover. When there was a drought and they needed rain, this man would move clouds or make clouds causing it to rain. Dr Dyer then says he wanted to embrace the idea or the notion that someone had that power or ability to alter natural forces, but there was that conditioned doubt that would prevent such a thing. It wasn't until he shifted his thinking to a more spiritual realm that he realized (and here was my wakeup call) that the same energy that moves a thought across my mind moves a cloud across the sky. There's only one. The same energy that opens a flower every morning beats my heart everyday, and the same energy that moves the planets throughout the galaxies can take a tiny seed and turn it into a human being. There's only one energy. If there is only one energy in the world, one universal force, that's in everything and is everywhere, and there is no place that it is not, then it's not outside the realm of even logic to assume that if it's in me and it's in the clouds and that if I could somehow banish the doubt regarding my ability to be able to use this same energy that's in the clouds that's in me to bring about precipitation, if I had that capacity... You must banish doubt.

It was at that moment that I remembered that I was one with this energy he was speaking of, and also at that moment I said, out loud, "I will not be sick anymore." A calm, peaceful feeling came over me, and I gently said, "I will not do this Epstein-Barr one minute longer. I am done with it." And just that quick it was over. What had been destroying my life since February was finally over, and not only was I over Epstein-Barr, but most importantly, I was back in contact with my Creator. I had taken Spirit to the disease, and the Spirit won.

I had known of God my entire life. I had been raised in church and had heard of God and taught all of the Bible's stories and teachings. I was gloriously saved by our Creator, God, at the age of nine. I had been taught that everyone needed this salvation and a personal testimony, but I now know it's more than that. Yes the salvation will prepare your soul for eternity, but what about the now? It's more than just going to church on Sunday or even every time the doors are open, not that there is anything wrong with that because if you are so led you should do that. As it says in Hebrews, we should not forsake the assembling of ourselves together; but, it needs to be a personal relationship. We need to be in constant contact with the Spirit. We need to dwell in the Spirit.

Before we continue, may I say that I'm not going to get religious with you, but I do want to get spiritual with you because that is what we are. We are spirit, and religion has nothing to do with it. Religion is a cause, principle, or system of beliefs held to with ardor and faith. So religion can be anything. It can be Christianity, Judaism, Buddhism, even atheism. It can be football, baseball, fishing, partying, even work, anything that you do regularly and put your trust in. What I want you to come to know is the Spirit and know the Spirit on a personal level.

What I was never taught is that we can actually call on and use this awesome force in our daily lives, to heal the sick, help those that are less fortunate, and create abundance for ourselves and others. Anything and everything we do, every step we take we should be spiritually minded. The Spirit is with us with every step we take, like it or not, so why not acknowledge it and take full advantage of it. In the book of Romans, it says, for to be carnally minded is death; but to be spiritually minded is life and peace. I chose life and peace, and that is exactly what it is. It is a choice. We make a choice in every second of every day. We make a choice to be happy or sad. We make a choice to be healthy or not. Let's face it. Everything is a choice. You may not think so. You may think, *well, I didn't make a choice to be sick. It runs in my family. There was just no way it was going to miss me.* Or you could be the one that thinks, *I always have bad luck. Nothing good ever happens to me.* This is what I'm talking about. You may not think of this as making a choice, but it is. Just because there have been many alcoholics in your family doesn't mean that you are going to be one as well. Just don't drink. It is really that simple. I don't mean to make little of those that have drinking problems or those that have disease that seems to run in the family. I definitely am not because I have been you. The very first chapter of this book shows exactly what I mean. I had made a choice, a conscious decision, to wonder what kind of illness or injury I would have next.

Also I had smoked cigarettes since I was sixteen years old, and on December 23, 2007 some twenty-five years later, I said, "I will no longer do this to my body, I took the Spirit to this addiction and stopped. I have had no cravings, no withdrawal symptoms, nothing.

The Spirit works. It's a living force, meaning its alive just like our spirit is alive, and it's here to work with our spirit for the good of all. If we so choose.

In the coming chapters, I will explain this Spirit who created us and every other living thing. Why we were created. How to establish initial contact with our Creator, how to maintain this contact through losing doubt, controlling the ego, and how to manifest abundance in your life through the spirit, all the while ridding yourself of any *dis* (disease, disharmony, discomfort, discord, etc.) you may have.

Initial Contact

(In the Beginning)

Before continuing, I would like to ask that you keep an open mind, if only for the time it takes to finish reading this book. There may be and probably will be things that you will read that may go against everything you have believed your entire life, but please keep an open mind. Not only that, open your heart and allow your spirit to commune with the Spirit and listen to what it is telling you.

We see in the New Testament it says, the Spirit itself beareth witness with our spirit. So please, from this point on read with the heart and not the head. Also, before we can talk about healing, help, comfort, and the ability to manifest things in our lives; we must first look at the One who is responsible for all of these things. As I said earlier, call him what you will, he has many names and with no disrespect for others, but in the following chapters I will refer to him as God, The One, Creator, Spirit, and universal force.

Let us start with the very beginning, as we all know, in the beginning God created the heavens and the earth. Genesis goes on to describe the order in which everything was created. Then we come to the part of Genesis that says, "And God said; Let us make man in our image, after our likeness" (Genesis 1:26). Let's look at this for just a moment because it is extremely important that you understand this. We must understand what this image is. Is God made of flesh and bone like we are? Does God have the same outward appearance that we do? *No.* He definitely does not, because as it says in John 4:24, God is a spirit, so if we were created after His image then we must be spirit as well, God's spirit. It also says in Revelation 1:8, "I am Alpha and Omega, the beginning and the ending, saith the Lord, which is, and which was, and which is to come, the Almighty." Reading this we see that not only is God a Spirit, He is eternal, as it says in Psalms; God is from everlasting to everlasting. Now then, if God is a spirit and eternal then we must be spirit and eternal as well.

We are only in the flesh for a short time but our spirit lives and has lived forever. Jesus said, It is the spirit that gives life; the flesh counts for nothing: the words that I speak unto you, they are spirit, and they are life. I would like for you to keep this in mind as we continue. Now let's look at the book of John for just a moment. Once again, I know your thinking, where in the world is he going with this? Well, I'll tell you. We are going to be talking about the healing power of the spirit; I don't believe we can talk about the healing power of the Spirit without talking about Jesus and how we receive this Spirit. Now John 1:1–4 says, "In the beginning," looks similar to Genesis 1:1, right? "In the beginning was the Word and the Word was with God and the Word was God. The same was in the beginning with God. All things were made by him; and without him was not any thing made that was made. In him was life; and the life was the light of men."

Jesus is our pathway to this spirit. Jesus said in John 14:6, "I am the way, the truth, and the life: no man cometh unto the Father, but by me." Also in the John 3:16–17, we find probably the most well known scripture in the Bible.

"For God so loved the world, that he gave his only begotten Son, that whosoever believeth in him should not perish, but have everlasting life. For God sent not his Son into the world to condemn the world; but that the world through him might be saved."

This is how we make initial contact with the spirit. This is the salvation I spoke of earlier. I was saved at nine years of age. My experience was this; I was at church (please know you do not have to be at church; God will save you anywhere you may be, in bed, in the bathtub, in a ditch, anywhere). We were having our annual revival meeting. The preacher was preaching the word of God, and in my heart I realized my condition that I had sinned. The Bible tells us in Romans 3:23, "For all have sinned, and come short of the glory of God"; I then made a choice to repent, that is to ask God to forgive me of my sin, and ask God to save my soul, and he did.

Let me explain, the realization I had in my heart was the drawing power of the Spirit, as Jesus said in John 6:44, "No man can come to me, except the Father which hath sent me draw him." It is God's Spirit that does the drawing, then upon repentance it is God that places the

Holy Spirit in our heart. All we must do is believe. God does the work as we see in Ephesians 2:8, "For by grace are ye saved through faith; and that not of yourselves: it is the gift of God." It is by God's grace through our believing in his Son, Jesus, that we are saved.

If there was a step-by-step guide to attaining this Spirit it would look like this:

1. *You hear the word of God.*

    This hearing could be someone talking to you, a book you are reading, a TV broadcast, a radio show, anyway that God's word is brought to you accompanied by the Spirit. This Spirit speaks to the heart and lets you know that you need God to come into your life. Let's look at the conversion of Paul (Saul, of Tarsus) for just a moment. Saul was on the road to Damascus to persecute Christians when God spoke to him. We find this event in Acts 9:3–4. "And as he [Saul] journeyed, he came near Damascus: and suddenly there shined round about him a light from heaven: And he fell to the earth, and heard a voice saying unto him, Saul, Saul, why persecutest thou me?"

    Here we see Saul heard the Word (this Word being Jesus), which leads to the next step.

2. *You realize your condition and that you need God.*

In Acts 9:5, of this story we see the Spirit dealing with Saul's heart. "And he said, Who art thou, Lord? And the Lord said, I am Jesus whom thou persecutest: it is hard for thee to kick against the pricks."

The kicking against the pricks is the Spirit dealing with Saul's heart (Paul later referred to this kicking against the pricks as godly sorrow, in 2 Corinthians 7:10. "For godly sorrow worketh repentance to salvation not to be repented of: but the sorrow of the world worketh death,"). This leads to step number three.

3. *You repent to God.*

Acts 9:6 states, "And he trembling and astonished said, Lord, what wilt thou have me to do?" We see here that Saul was afraid (he was trembling and astonished) his repentance was the fact that he was willing to do anything that God would have him do. This is how we all must be. We must be willing. One can repent silently, or say out loud, "Lord, forgive me," but if it is not sincere from the heart He will not hear us. On the other hand, when we repent with the heart that Saul displays in this passage, salvation is instant. Step number four is not really a step once step number three takes place, God does the rest. All we must do is believe.

4. *God will save your soul.*

(The remainder of Acts 9:6) "...And the Lord said unto him, Arise, and go into the city, and it shall be told thee what thou must do." I believe it was here, when Christ said "Arise," that Saul was saved. Now for Paul it seemed to be instant, he repented and God spoke peace to him. Do not be discouraged if it does not work that easily for you. I have known and heard of people that try to repent time and time again with no success. Like I said in step three, we must be willing and have faith (Faith means having no doubt) that God will send His Spirit into our heart. When these conditions are met, the very instant they are met, the ever calming peace of the Spirit will come into our heart.

Note: Some people may struggle with this repentance to God, but let me assure you, it is *the* most important thing you will ever do while on this earth.

Buddha said that the most important thing you can do in your life is to come to know something that cannot be destroyed by death. There is only One that I'm aware of that cannot be destroyed by death. That is God.

There are multiple things that hinder our acceptance and service to our Creator and can cause us all kinds of difficulty as we go through life. Two of which are our doubt and ego.

Doubt

Let's look at our doubt for a moment: what it is, and how it affects our life.

Webster's describes doubt as, "fear, a lack of confidence, to consider unlikely or uncertainty of belief or opinion that often interferes with decision-making." Doubt affects every aspect of our life. We have been taught this, inadvertently, by our parents, peers, and even the events of our life.

I read a story of a cancer patient that was in his last hours on this earth. The doctors had given up all hope, and he wasn't going to make it through the weekend. This patient had heard of an experimental medicine and had been asking his doctors for it. They had been declining to prescribe it to him knowing that he was not going to make it. However, at the last minute his doctor decided, what difference would it make, he wasn't going to make it anyway, I might as well honor my patient's last request.

Now, this guy was never supposed to leave the hospital. He was administered a shot of this new medicine on Saturday and was walking out, going home on Sunday.

Two months later, our "cancer-free" patient was watching a news broadcast and they were airing a special on this new cancer medication that was a flop. This medication was the same that he had been taking, and guess what? The next day he was back in the hospital with the same diagnosis as before, terminal cancer, and he was not going to make it back home.

His doctor, realizing what was going on, told him that what the news did not say was that there was a newer version of that medication just released, and he had it. The doctor administered an injection of this new version of the medication and the next day the patient walked out of the hospital, once again with no ill effects of cancer. The patient didn't know that his doctor had given him a shot of saline and nothing more.

Two or three months pass and there was another news special regarding this "new medication," and that there was no mistake that it was definitely a total failure and could not do anything for cancer. The patient saw this and two days later was dead.

What I would like for you to see in this is this gentlemen's doubt, when he didn't doubt he was fine. As long as he was knowing (knowing means an absence of doubt) he was fine. But, the very moment he started to have doubt it would affect his life and would eventually kill him.

We can do miraculous things when we banish doubt. Jesus says in the book of Mark 11:23, "For verily I say unto you, That whosoever shall say unto this mountain, Be thou removed, and be thou cast into the sea; and shall not *doubt* in his heart, but shall believe that those things which he saith shall come to pass; he shall have whatsoever he saith."

Jesus also said in Matthew's writing, "And all things, whatsoever ye shall ask in prayer, *believing*, ye shall receive" (Matthew 21:22). Lose the doubt and have anything you wish. No kidding! We will speak of this more in the chapter titled "Manifesting."

Ego

Now let's take look at the ego and see what kind of chaos it can cause.

Gary S. Hall

Here is how Webster's defines the ego:

1. the self especially as contrasted with another self or the world
2. a: egotism b: self-esteem
3. the one of the three divisions of the psyche in psychoanalytic theory that serves as the organized conscious mediator between the person and reality especially by functioning both in the perception of and adaptation to reality.

The ego I am speaking of is that other self. The voice inside your head that says you must always be right. You must look a certain way. You must act a certain way. You must have a good job. You must have lots of money. You must hang around a certain group of people.

Most people believe that these are the things that make up who they are. But they are not, they are our ego. They are things that we have mistaken for ourselves. Almost all of us do this. We do not know any better and haven't been taught any better. You can ask anybody who they are and more than likely they will define themselves by their name, race, color, gender, or job. But, this is not who we are. These are only some of the things that we do and they cover up who and what we really are.

I will speak of my own ego and what it has done for me. In my early twenties, my ego got so out of hand that it cost me a small fortune, family, and just about killed me. I started a mobile automotive detail business in Nashville, Tennessee at the age of twenty-one. At twenty-two, I met a gentleman from Louisville, Kentucky with the same aspiration. I moved my business to Louisville and became partners with this gentleman. Business was great and the money was flowing (this was something else I was never taught about, money management, not that it would have mattered because my ego was running a thousand miles an hour). The automotive detail business turned into a limousine buying and selling fiasco.

My partner and I had one of the largest houses in our subdivision; we had two chauffeurs that lived with us full time. We would have crazy parties and had an entourage that seemed to follow us everywhere we went. We were thinking and living like rock stars. We got to where we would sleep until noon, working maybe a couple hours a day or not at all, start partying again at five o'clock and the cycle would start over. We were killing ourselves physically and spiritually but the ego kept saying, *Oh, its okay, you need those limos, you need all of those friends, you'll make more money, you can make it up to your family, it will be all right, and what will people think if you didn't have all of these things.* Well, the ego would say, *You would be a loser.*

Well, to make a long story short. I was ego driven until I had lost everything, and I mean everything. Houses, vehicles, boats, you know, a whole lot of material stuff, but worst of all I had permanently hurt what mattered most in my life, my family. I wound up sick and found myself in a hospital in Nashville having the lower lobe of my left lung removed after a mass had been detected by a CAT scan.

It was a crazy time in my life, one day I was riding around in a chauffeur driven Mercedes 500 SEL Stretch limousine, one of two in the United States, and the next I was riding a ten speed bike that wasn't even mine.

My ego was the driving force in my life and being spiritually minded was totally absent from my life and not even a thought process, every thought was carnal, and what does the Bible say about being carnally minded? To be carnally minded is *death*. On this occasion the ego had just about taken my life but, this universal force, the Spirit, which I have been speaking of, had other intentions.

In losing doubt and controlling the ego it is easier to be spiritually minded and therefore having life and peace.

Our Past

There is another issue that we as humans have that can hinder our service and acceptance of the Source, and not only that but also it will hinder us in every aspect of our lives. It is our history, our past. You know the baggage that we pick up and collect as we go through life. This baggage is our personal experiences, and we think we are required to keep all of these things regardless of how bad they may be. We take this history into every situation and every decision we make. I touched on this in a previous chapter by referring to a person who has sickness or dis-ease that seems to run in the family, but it doesn't necessarily have to be dis-ease or sickness it could be, as I had, an addiction to smoking cigarettes. I had smoked so long, twenty-five years, I doubted I could ever quit, why? Because that was my history, it is just what I had done for so many years of my life I couldn't see myself changing. In the first chapter, my "now" was spent, probably just like many of you, thinking of what was going to happen next, *Would I be sick? Would I get injured? Or what kind of surgery would I have?* Why? I have had many family members die of cancer and for years thought that I would contract cancer as well. I have also heard countless people say I am going to have this pain or that dis-ease because it runs in the family it is only a matter of time before I get it. *No it is not!*

Declare right now, to stop living in the past. If you want better health, declare better health and take the Spirit to it. Want to stop smoking, declare it, and take the Spirit to it and stop. Say out loud or in the calm of your own heart and mind to whatever it may be that is hindering you to stop. You can do it! Reclaim dominion and leave the past in its proper place, and where it already is—*behind you.*

We must shift our thinking from the past to the "now." The past is just exactly that, the past. It has no relevance to the "now," except that which you give it. Let it go. Turn to God and take the Spirit to whatever it is that may be hindering you.

Maintaining Contact

(Spiritual Maintenance)

The key is to stay spiritually minded, as I mentioned in the last chapter, being spiritually minded is life and peace. It is really that simple. However, I know that during the course of everyday living it can be tough sometimes to stay focused and stay in this mindset. I have found that for me, it is best to start my day with prayer and meditation and to keep myself surrounded by positive things and positive people.

I will keep a Bible and some other spiritual books on my desk; right now, I have a book by Deepak Chopra, *The Seven Spiritual Laws of Success*. I try to listen to positive and uplifting music. I try to keep my language positive, and I also try to do good things for others, by doing this, it seems to rub off on those around me thereby keeping them positive as well.

Doing good deeds, I believe this is why we are here on this earth, to serve others; Your Creator did not put you where you are at, at this moment, just to be there. We have a purpose. Each one of us has a purpose. I suggest, as Linn Strouse made the suggestion to me, you find out what your purpose is and while doing so, do good deeds. The benefit is absolutely unbelievable. There have been many scientific studies that prove this. Not only are we supposed to do good things as it says in the book of Ephesians 2:10, "For we are his workmanship, created in Christ Jesus unto good works, which God hath before ordained that we should walk in them," but we will be happier and healthier for doing so. Studies have shown that not only the recipient is affected in a positive way but also the one doing the good deed will have major benefits as well, even someone that observes a good deed being done to someone else has the same benefits. Lower stress levels, increased immune function you get the idea, it is a win for all involved.

I believe my purpose is this, as Jesus says in the New Testament,

Gary S. Hall

All power is given unto me in heaven and in earth. Go ye therefore, and teach all nations, baptizing them in the name of the Father, and of the Son, and of the Holy Ghost: Teaching them to observe all things whatsoever I have commanded you: and, lo, I am with you always, even unto the end of the world. Amen.

Matthew 28:18–20

These verses of scripture are also known as The Great Commission. You do not have to be a preacher, a member of a church, or anything of the like. As it says, we *all* must "go ye and teach," and let us not forget the "therefore," the "therefore" is referencing the power that was given to Jesus on earth and in heaven. This same power is ours. God gives us this power through the Spirit to "go ye therefore, and teach all nations." All nations in your case may be your own home, where you work, where you live, or halfway around the world, only you and the Spirit know. As Linn Strouse asked me, I ask you, what is your purpose? Don't know? Figure it out!

Here is a step by step guide for what I call maintaining Contact or Spiritual Maintenance found in the New Testament:

1. *Rejoice evermore*: "Rejoice" meaning to be happy or full of joy and "evermore" meaning, always and or forever. Here we see we should always be happy, and yes, this means even during the tough times. Keep in mind that the tough times will not be as tough if we are connected with the Source and are spiritually minded.

2. *Pray without ceasing*: I don't believe this means to stay kneeled down in prayer constantly. Not that we do not need to spend ample time in prayer because we do. I start my day with twenty to thirty minutes of prayer and meditation. Some days may require more than others. As Jesus said, in Matthew 26:41 "The Spirit is indeed willing but the flesh is weak." Okay, so most days twenty to thirty minutes in the morning is just not enough. This is why it says pray without ceasing, meaning, we should keep God in our consciousness constantly. In any situation, see God in it. In any situation and in everything we do, in every second of every day, we should have this consciousness. God consciousness. This is that higher level of consciousness we have spoke of. So this pray without ceasing is not asking God to constantly do something for us; rather, it is the awareness that we must have that God has already accomplished it. So this is the mindset we must constantly strive to stay in. Stay spiritually minded.

All day. Every day. Also, as it said in regards to rejoicing, pray without ceasing *evermore*.

3. *In everything give thanks: for this is the will of God in Christ Jesus concerning you*: This is pretty self explanatory, give thanks and be grateful for everything that has been made manifest in your life. We should do this every day. This is one of those things that should be included in our daily praying without ceasing. We have so much to be grateful for regardless of our situations at the moment. Life is full of blessings just waiting for us to recognize and acknowledge them. Be grateful and practice gratitude daily. In everything give thanks.

4. *Quench not the Spirit*: This could also read, despise not the Spirit, or suppress not the Spirit. Anyway, we have been talking about staying spiritually minded, maintaining a higher level of consciousness or God consciousness and pray without ceasing, right? Well, when you begin to do these things the Spirit begins to communicate with you. Some of you may now be thinking, *Yep, he's lost it*. But really, as you begin to pray without ceasing and staying in a more spiritual mindset, the Spirit begins to commune with your spirit. It may be during your first prayer of the morning or during meditation; it may be while driving down the road; or during a conversation with a friend or colleague; the Spirit will

begin giving you direction in your life, leading, if you will allow It to. Please allow the Spirit to lead your life, don't suppress it or quench it. Thirst for it and listen to what it is telling you.

5. *Know that God is a rewarder of those that diligently seek him*: Constantly seek His will for your life. It says in Hebrews 11:6, "But without faith it is impossible to please him: for he that cometh to God must believe that he is, and that he is a rewarder of them that diligently seek him." First, we see that without *faith* it is impossible to please Him. We can have no doubt. Doubt has no place in our lives. Then I want you to see that He is a rewarder of them that diligently seek Him. Not that He is going to give you a prize for seeking Him, but through the seeking we find, we find life, we find happiness, we find health, we find abundance, we find that He is our sufficiency. That is our reward. When we make a conscious decision to seek, *knowing* we will find, is when we will begin to see things happen. As Joel Goldsmith said, "Remember this—it is the recognition and acknowledgement of the presence of God that brings God into tangible evidence, manifestation, and expression."

Now, let's look at "diligent," meaning steady or steadfast, constantly. If we will do this, seek Him diligently, He will first save our soul, and secondly, (here is where help, healing, and comfort come in) He will help you create in your life anything you can possibly imagine. Remember this also, "all things work together for good to them that love God, to them who are the called according to his purpose," (Romans 8:28).

By and through this "Maintaining Contact (Spiritual Maintenance)" we can come to know what our individual purpose is and live a life more abundant.

Prayer/Meditation

(Making Contact with God)

We have all heard of prayer, and for the most part all of us have prayed. Some will say that prayer and meditation are the same thing and that's okay as long as you make time to talk to God and most importantly, take time to listen, as He says, "Be still and know that I am God" (Psalm 46:10).

As I stated in a previous chapter, I started to meditate in August of 2007. I had purchased a home study course from the Silva Ultra Mind Web site, and from the very first time I tried it, I had amazing results. I practiced daily, several times daily as a matter a fact. It was a huge help and many of the techniques I learned

I still use today. The Daisy Pond, a relaxation meditation, is my favorite.

Then in December, after listening to Dr. Dyer's, *Secrets of your own Healing Power*, I started Japa, which is a meditation where you're repeating of the sound of God. This is a morning and evening meditation. The morning meditation is a creation meditation and the evening meditation is a gratitude meditation.

In the morning I meditate on the things I wish to manifest in my life and the lives of others, also I have daily affirmations that I repeat, all while repeating the sound of God. That sound being, Ah. The evening meditation, the gratitude meditation, we repeat the sound of thanksgiving or peace, this sound is ohm…during this meditation we give thanks for things that have been made manifest in our lives this day.

I do not want to rewrite Dr. Dyer's book, so I won't, but I will suggest that you buy it. It is called *Getting in the Gap* and includes a CD that explains this meditation technique and will also guide you through the morning and evening meditations.

After you make your initial contact with the Creator, if you try or get nothing else out of this book, I suggest, no, I plead with you, try this meditation. I

Gary S. Hall

am one hundred percent confident that if you do, great things will begin to happen in your life.

Through prayer and meditation is how we stay one with the Spirit and maintain conscious contact with God. When we acknowledge and are receptive to our connection to the Spirit is when we begin to see incredible things happen in our lives and the lives of others. As we are told by our Creator, "Be still, and know that I am God."

Please, take a few minutes out of each day, slow down, slow your mind down, be still, and listen to what the Spirit is telling you. The Spirit will lead, guide, and direct us in every aspect of our lives, and all we must do is be receptive to it. As I have said, "all things work together for good to them that love God." This is that Spirit working in everything for you. The Spirit, this universal force is talking to you, are you listening?

Manifesting

(Co-Creating your life)

I would like to start this chapter by looking back at my thoughts in the first chapter, "As You Think So Shall You Be." There has never been a more true statement. Look at your life, and you tell me, are you a product of your thoughts? If you are being honest, the answer will be an absolute yes! Negative or positive, whichever way you tend to think is how you will live.

If you continually think negative thoughts, regardless of what they are, the negative will happen. It has been my experience that my thoughts have had an effect in every aspect of my life, from work to personal, and yes, even to spiritual. For example, the funny, or not so funny, thing about a negative thought is that you might have a negative thought or idea about someone or something at work and before you know it that little negativity has spread to your personal life as well. Negative thinking is like a cancer; it can become all-consuming if allowed too. Notice I said if allowed too, we have the ability to control, our thinking. I spoke earlier of a making a choice. Just as we make a choice when driving, to turn right or left, drive the speed limit or not, we make a choice every second of every day we live. We choose what we shall think, be it good or bad. We actually choose to be healthy or not. We choose to have abundance or not. We have been given, from our Creator, a freewill, which means we choose what we will do with our life, every second of every minute of every hour, you get the idea; we choose everything. If you continually think I don't like what is going on in my life right now, regardless of what it is, it will continue to manifest itself in your life because that is what you are bringing to yourself. The Spirit or the one universal force is just working with you giving you what you are creating. We must come to realize that this spirit or this universal force is a part of us, and we are co-creators with this Spirit, meaning we co-create everything in our life. Believe it or not, it is true.

If you want things to be better in your life, let them be better. I don't mean wish or pray that you want things to be better, because then you will always be wanting and never having. Joel Goldsmith, a Christian scientist who has written numerous books including: *The Infinite Way*, *Our Spiritual Resources* and too many more to list, tells us that it is a foolish mission to ask God or try to persuade God into doing something for us, as if he is holding something back or not allowing us to have it. God is forever creating. God is forever blessing. Goldsmith also writes in *Living the Infinite Way,* "that it is the recognition and acknowledgement of the presence of God that brings God into tangible evidence, manifestation, and expression."

We must come to the realization that God is in us, and we are in God. It says in I John 4:4, "Greater is He that is in you, than He that is in the world" Also as Jesus said in John 15:7, "If ye abide in me, and my words abide in you, ye shall ask what ye will, and it shall be done unto you."

After our initial contact with God, we must know that the Spirit is our companion. Remember it is with us every step we take, like it or not, and works for us. Not only God's Spirit, but all spirit, other people, events, anything you can imagine. In Romans 8:28, we read, "And we know that all things work together for good to them that love God."

You may be getting tired of hearing this, but I have no doubt that this is the case. Since I have been writing this book, it seems like everything has contributed to it in some shape, form, or fashion. I can be at church and hear a verse of Scripture, and it is the verse I had been thinking of or looking for. I can be at work and someone will say just the right thing, or they may be looking for some assistance with a problem of their own, and the right thing to say just pops into my mind. Even the postal service has given guidance.

While I was writing the first chapter of this book, I had hit a wall. I was looking for a statement made by Buddha and couldn't find it. I knew it, but I wanted it to be exact. I had looked in every book that I have and on the Internet, I just could not find it. So I thought I would take a short break from my writing and go check the mail. Guess what? I couldn't believe it. I opened a letter from a writer's newsletter group I am a member of and inside was this card that had absolutely nothing to do with the newsletter. This small card read, "All that we are is the result of what we have thought. The mind is everything. What we think, we become" (Buddha). This is that all-powerful Spirit that I'm talking about.

Knowing this, let's look at positive thinking. Now, I'm not talking about goal setting and action steps. I'm talking about a "knowing," meaning having no doubt. Seeing things from the end, meaning, see and think of things the way you know they will be. During my morning meditation, I see things I want to manifest in my life and in the lives of others, either for that day or maybe even long-term ideas. (You might think, *I'm losing it here,* but hang in here with me.) Once I have shared these things with the Spirit or universal force, I let it go. I don't try to force anything or let my ego get in the way by saying or thinking things should work like this or like that and have some kind of preconceived notion as to an order of things. You must know that the Spirit will work out all of the details. We are told this in Isaiah 45:2, I will go before thee, and make the crooked places straight: This is God telling us that wherever we may be going He has already been there to work out all of the details.

We have talked about doubt in a previous chapter, but now let's look at removing this doubt. This can be quite

A Wake Up Call

difficult for some because the majority of us have been raised with doubt. From birth, we have been taught limitations from our parents, you can't do this or you can't do that, or that can be done by only those who have lots of money or that can only be done by those that have a certain skill set. Not that this was their fault because they were raised with this doubt as well. Doubt will hinder us, and as a matter of fact, it will stop you before you ever get started. What we must do is rid ourselves of doubt. We do this by thinking positive, talking positive, living positive, meditating, and staying in constant contact with our Creator. As soon as a negative thought enters into your consciousness, stop it and turn it into a positive, and also as a negative situation or problem confronts you, look at the big picture and see how it fits into the grand scheme of things. This negative or problem may be the guidance you have been looking for, so don't fight it, flow with it. And know that Spirit will work out all of the details.

This will take some work, but as you start to see the positive change in your life, it will get easier, and most importantly, you will begin looking for positive things to happen out of bad or what you had previously thought as a bad situation, and they will. As we get closer and more in tune with the Spirit, the one universal force, things will just start happening.

I know some may think, and I have heard some say that they think that our Creator is a mean kid with a magnifying glass, and we are a bunch of ants. Please, I beg to differ. Our Creator, God, is love, and it tells us this in 1 John 4 (this chapter also says we should love one another). This is true, God wants us to have a great life, and all we have to do is believe that He wants us to have a great life. Jesus said through Matthew's writing, "Ask, and it shall be given you; seek, and ye shall find; knock, and it shall be opened unto you: For every one that asketh receiveth; and he that seeketh findeth; and to him that knocketh it shall be opened," (Matthew 7:7–8).

We see here that all we have to do is go get it, whatever that may be for you, go get it. I mean *take it*. It is there for you. What is it that you desire? Do you want better physical health, better emotional health, more money, a better job; it does not matter whatever it may be it is yours.

Do you have children? Do you not want the best for them? Do you not go out of your way to make sure they can have and do whatever it is they want, and do you not want better things for them than you had yourself? This is the way that God feels toward us. Let's now look at the remainder of this passage, Jesus goes on to say, "Or what man is there of you, whom if his son ask bread, will he give him a stone? Or if he asks a fish, will he give him a serpent? If ye then, being evil, know how to give good gifts unto your children, how much more shall your Father which is in heaven give good things to them that ask Him?" (Matthew 7:9–11).

Paul says in Romans that we are children of God, and if children, then heirs; heirs of God, and joint-heirs with Christ; Now, come on, how powerful is that. Think about it, it is saying we are joint-heirs with Christ. We spoke earlier of Jesus speaking in Matthew regarding all power was given to Him, Jesus, in heaven and earth. Then we saw what Jesus said, "If ye abide in me, and my words abide in you, ye shall ask what ye will, and it shall be done unto you."

This is why I wrote previously that the Spirit or the one universal force is working for us and wants us to have whatever it is that we desire. All we must do is believe (*no doubting*). You may be getting tired of hearing this believe without doubting stuff, but it is imperative that we lose the doubt and ego and shift our thinking to a more spiritual mindset. Always remember, to be spiritually minded is life and peace. Also remember, Jesus said it is the Spirit that gives life and the flesh counts for nothing. This is why we must stay spiritually minded because the flesh, carnal mind, or ego, however you want to put it, counts for nothing.

In a previous chapter, I spoke of Dr. Dyer shifting his thinking to a more spiritual realm, and I also spoke of a higher consciousness or God consciousness. This is what we must do, we must think on a higher plane. If you want better health, you don't need to be thinking about how sick you are.

If you continually think or give power to sickness that is exactly what you will continue to bring to yourself—sickness. Go to the source and *be* better health. Shift your thinking and give your energy to that which is positive, be spiritually minded. Take the Spirit to whatever problem or dis- you are having and I guarantee you that it will vanish.

Keep in mind there are things you have to do as well. You cannot want better health and eat at McDonalds every meal, smoke cigarettes like a freight train, stay out drinking, and partying all night long. Common sense ought to tell you that that is not good for you, but you know what? Thousands of people do all of these things everyday and wonder, *Why do I feel bad*? *Why am I so sick*? Sounds crazy doesn't it? But, most of us have done this.

If you want better health, *be* better health. Go to the Source and have better health. As I stated earlier, we are in God, God is in us and God is good. There is no sickness in God. There is no dis-ease in God. There is no dis-anything in God. If it is good, it is of God. If it is not good, it is of us. So with sickness or whatever dis you may have, it has no power over you, as a matter of fact, it only exists because you allow it to.

Joel Goldsmith, in his book, *The Foundations of Mysticism*, relates a story of Christ and a cripple man. Christ asks, "What did hinder you? Rise, take up your bed and walk." Goldsmith goes on to say, that's an astonishing statement. Here's a cripple man and he's asked, "What did hinder you?" Common sense would have said, "I'm crippled, that's what's hindering me." But Jesus saw that and still said, "What did hinder you? Rise, pick up your bed and walk." In other words, that which is binding you isn't power; you are bound by your acceptance of it as power.

The problem is that we have gotten disconnected from our source. We have put our faith or trust in doctors or in this medication or that medication. Every other commercial on television or advertisement in magazines are for this drug or that drug.

Do you want to lose weight? Take this pill. Do

you want to lower your blood pressure? Take this pill. Lower your cholesterol? Having mood swing issues? Are you depressed? Are you ill? So you have a dis? Take a pill. Whatever the want may be, most people want to take a pill to get over it. People think this way because it seems to be quick and immediate relief from whatever the dis may be, or should I say, it is the easy way. Everyone is looking for the easy way out, Oh, maybe I can take a pill for that.

As I talked about in the chapter "Epstein-Barr (A Search for a Cure)," I was taking handfuls of vitamins, minerals, and herbs; and you know what? It wasn't instant, as a matter of fact, it wasn't easy. I had been taking these things for months. I had spent thousands of dollars on doctors, treatments, and pills. But the moment, the very instant, I returned to the source, I was healed. There was no time lapse, no recovery period. It was instant. And, it was free.

As Jesus tells us in the New Testament, "Son, thou art ever with me, and all that I have is thine," (Luke 15:31). Be it health, abundance, or whatever we wish in life; it is already ours. It has been given to us by the master. All we have to do is claim it. Reclaim the dominion that God has given us. And remember, as Christ tells us, "And all things, whatsoever ye shall ask in prayer, *believing*, ye shall receive." What more could you want, and what more do you need to know? Take the Spirit to whatever dis-ease, dis-harmony, dis-cord, and anything else in your life that is need of repair and have a life more abundant.

Remember, Read, Believe, and Live (Well).

Bibliography

Merriam-Webster Dictionary. Massachusetts: Merriam-Webster Dictionary, Inc., 2005.

Goldsmith, Joel. *Living the Infinite Way*. New York: Harper & Row, 1961.

————*The Foundations of Mysticism*. New York: Acropolis Books, 1998.

Notes:

Notes:

Notes:

Notes:

Notes:

Notes:

Notes:

Notes:

Notes:

Notes:

Notes:

Notes:

Notes:

Notes:

ORDER INFORMATION

To order additional copies of this book, please visit
www.redemption-press.com.
Also available on Amazon.com and BarnesandNoble.com
Or by calling toll free 1-844-2REDEEM.

CPSIA information can be obtained
at www.ICGtesting.com
Printed in the USA
BVOW06s1354261217
503650BV00026B/1318/P